Short *ish* Walks

near Yorkshire's

Three Peaks

Paul White

Whinray Books • Ilkley

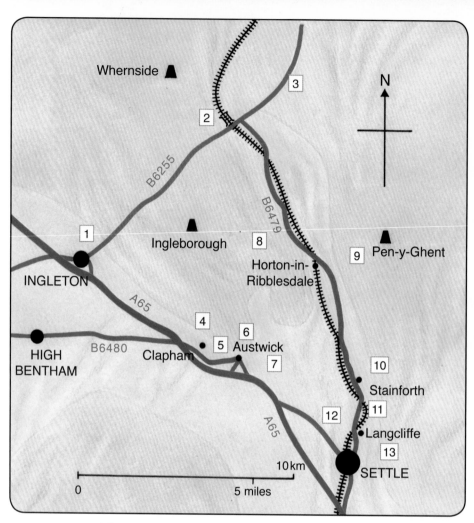

The approximate locations of the walks in this book

First published 2012 by Whinray Books,
an imprint of Bossiney Books Ltd, 33 Queens Drive, Ilkley, LS29 9QW
www.bossineybooks.com

ISBN 978-0-9571939-1-8

Acknowledgements
The maps are by Graham Hallowell. All photographs are by the author.
Cover based on a design by Heards Design Partnership.
The boots on the front cover were kindly supplied by The Brasher Boot Company.

Printed in Great Britain by R Booth Ltd, Penryn, Cornwall

2

Introduction

These 'shortish' walks are circular, typically 6.5-9km (4-6 miles) in length, and will take a morning or an afternoon. The exact time will vary according to your fitness, weather conditions, and how interested you are in what you see. As well as the 13 'shortish walks', we have included preferred routes for ascending Ingleborough and Whernside.

The Three Peaks area is an extraordinary landscape, renowned among geologists for its limestone, shaped by the Craven Fault system and by repeated glaciation. For me, it's a place of childhood memories and the knowledge that my ancestors farmed here over many centuries. There are plenty of abandoned or converted farms, ruined barns and tottering stone walls which give a glimpse of an ancient and very tough way of life – not altogether gone, because there are still many working farms, especially in the lower pastureland.

To understand the area better, I recommend David Johnson's book *Ingleborough, Landscape and History* (Carnegie Publishing, 2008).

Safety (please take seriously!)

I don't want to be over-dramatic, but this area can be tricky, even dangerous. If you are safety-conscious you will probably have no problems, but you definitely need to go prepared. Some of these walks will take you into lonely places where mobile phones get no reception. Consult the weather forecast before you start, walk in company, let someone know where you are going. The maps in this book will be adequate for normal walking but may be of little use if you lose your bearings, so do take a proper map with you, such as the Ordnance Survey 1:25,000, as well as a compass and a GPS if you have one.

You will need proper walking boots or shoes for grip and ankle support. Many walkers find a walking pole is a helpful accessory. The high ground will always be colder than the lowlands and wind chill is often a factor. You should always carry extra clothing in your rucksack as well as waterproofs. Hat and gloves may well be needed (sunhat in summer) and you should take a good supply of water, because dehydration makes you tired, and some spare food.

Consideration for the landscape and for farmers

Please keep to the paths. Keep dogs on leads especially during the lambing and nesting seasons. Leave gates as you find them.

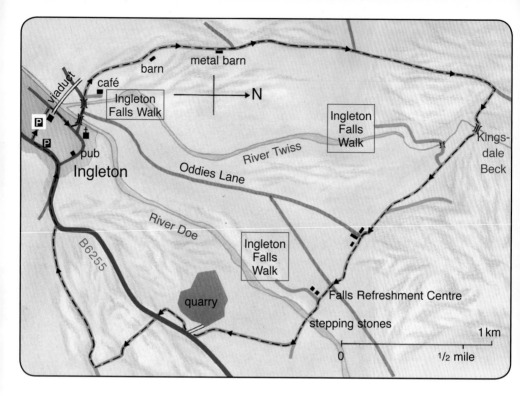

Walk 1   An Ingleton circuit

Distance: 9 km (5 1/2 miles)
Time: 2 1/4 hours
Character: This is a free alternative to the famous water-falls walk, with magnificent views of the countryside north of Ingleton. Fairly easy, though with some steady ascents. Some road walking. The stepping stones are impassable when the river is high, in which case use Oddies Lane as the return route.

Start from the Community Centre in the main car park. Take the road downhill (WATERFALLS WALK/VILLAGE CENTRE) and turn right under the disused railway viaduct.

Bear left downhill, and left again across two streams. Just outside the Ingleton Waterfalls Trail, continue ahead over a stile (THORNTON HALL). Cross an old railway track bed. Keep the wall on your right to a stile in the far right corner of the field, cross it and head to the left of a metal barn.

Turn right up the lane, which makes a long gentle ascent, with views of Ingleborough to the right. At the crown of the hill views of Kingsdale and Whernside open up. At the foot of a slope turn right on a broad track. Cross the Kingsdale Beck (soon mysteriously to become the River Twiss) and continue on the track to a farm. Take the stony track ahead (PUBLIC FOOTPATH).

Cross Oddies Lane. Just by the Falls Refreshment Centre, bear left downhill. Cross the stepping stones and continue ahead towards White Scar Cave. At a fork bear right, to a field gate with a pedestrian gate beside it. Bear right up the green track to a ladder stile at the far top corner of the field.

An enclosed track leads past the quarry entrance to the road. Cross the quarry access road and go through a pedestrian gate, following the path in a loop back to the main road.

Cross the road and a ladder stile (FELL LANE) and climb steadily with the wall on your left to a ladder stile, then with the wall on your right till you reach a major track – the main route to Ingleborough. Turn right, and walk back down to Ingleton.

Join the main road (care needed). Follow it when it bends to the left, past a car park. Then turn right into the main car park.

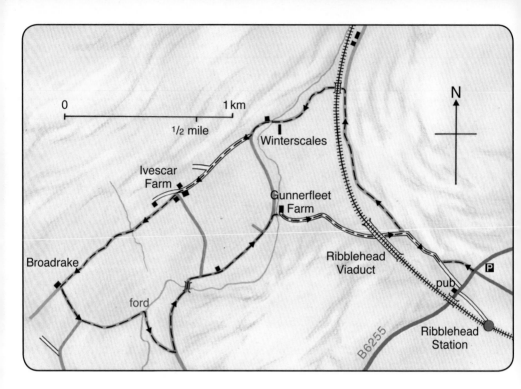

Walk 2   Ribblehead

Distance: 7.2km (4½ miles)   Time: 1¾ hours
Character: An easy almost flat walk in the level valley between Ingleborough and Whernside, with views of the famous Ribblehead Viaduct.

Park at the road junction near Ribblehead Viaduct (SD 766793) – or travel on the Settle & Carlisle Railway to Ribblehead Station. Take the peaty track towards the viaduct. Join a farm track.

Building the viaduct

From 1870 to 1875 a temporary community of around 2000 people lived in huts in the area to the east of the viaduct – an area jokingly called 'Sebastopol', with the management families housed nearby in 'Belgravia'. There were also brick-works and other industrial workings. The remains of these settlements are still visible as disturbed ground.

Don't turn left under the viaduct, but continue ahead (FP WHERNSIDE) with the railway on your left.

Beside a railway signal at Bleamoor Sidings, turn left (BRIDLE-WAY) under the railway. Follow the stony track past Winterscales Farm, then continue ahead (SCAR END) and ignore side turns.

At Ivescar Farm, go through the farmyard then continue ahead on a path across fields. Cross a stream by a plank bridge and bear right to a pedestrian gate, and then two more pedestrian gates.

At the next farm turn left down a farm track. When the track bears right across a cattle grid, leave it and continue ahead across open ground. Follow waymarks and an old track to a ford – bone dry when I crossed. Cross the river bed and head south, then after 100m veer south-east to a tarmac track with a gate and cattle grid. Turn left along the track.

After a bridge, fork right. At the farm, turn right across a bridge, RIBBLEHEAD. Join a stony track which leads under the viaduct, then retrace your steps to your car or the station.

There is a pub near the station, should you need refreshment.

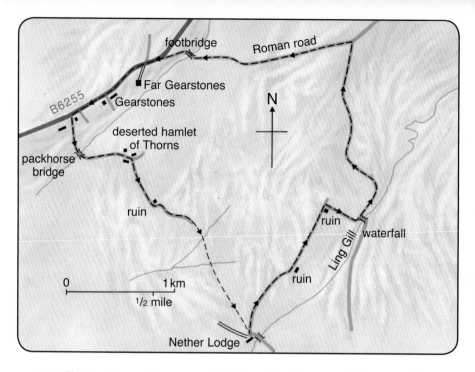

Walk 3   Gearstones to Nether Lodge and Ling Gill

Distance: 9.2km (5³/₄ miles)   Time: 2¹/₂ hours
Character: A very lonely moorland walk, often out of sight of habitation and on little walked paths. You are likely to get your feet wet. Compass and map essential. You will pass a number of deserted farms, and the general impression is of a landscape from which people have withdrawn.

Park on the roadside just west of Gearstones (SD778799). Walk west down the road, past a barn, then turn left (FP NETHER LODGE). Keep the wall on your left.

After crossing a lovely unspoiled packhorse bridge, bear left diagonally up the slope. At the top, bear right to a clump of trees containing the ruins of Thorns, a deserted settlement.

At the junction turn left then immediately right (FP NETHER LODGE). Cross the ladder stile then keep the wall on your left till you reach another ruin. Turn left into its yard and cross a stile, then follow the path.

You are now on the open moor, and the path is not always

clear, so head towards Pen-y-Ghent – approximately 150°. Cross two streams. Go through a gate, then head for Nether Lodge Farm ('lodges' were originally owned by monasteries, in this case Furness Abbey).

At the junction in front of the farm, turn sharp left (FP CAM END). Keep the wall on your right till you reach a stile: cross, then keep the fence on your left.

The trees mark another deserted farm. Now keep the wall on your right again. At a ladder stile by a ruined barn, turn right (LING GILL BRIDGE) and keep the wall on your right.

(On reaching a bridge, you might want to divert right briefly to look at Ling Gill Nature Reserve: the beck drops 30 m here, and you can hear the waterfall but alas not see it!)

Otherwise, continue with the stream on your right, along what is now a stony track. This climbs steadily to a T-junction. Turn left along the line of a Roman road, which was used as a turnpike road between 1751 and 1795.

After 1.5 km (or MXIV *passus* if you're a legionary) cross the Gayle Beck by a footbridge then join the Hawes-Ingleton road, passing the Gearstones Outdoor Centre and back to your car.

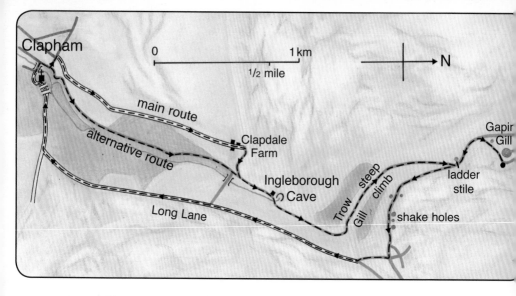

Walk 4 Clapdale and Gaping Gill

Distance: 8.8km (5 1/2 miles) but can be shortened
Time: 2 1/4 hours
Character: Two long steady ascents, and one steep rocky clamber
in Trow Gill, which are more than compensated for by the
scenery. Take a compass and map for safety on the moorland.

Start from the church at Clapham. Walk down to cross the
stream and turn right. At the entrance to the Ingleborough
Estate turn left, then after 80 m turn right on a track and follow
this up to Clapdale Farm. Go through the farmyard and immediately turn right downhill (INGLEBOROUGH CAVE).

At the foot of the slope, turn left onto the main path. Pass
Ingleborough Cave (a show cave with an impressive array of sta-
lactites) where the stream which plunges underground at Gaping
Gill returns to the daylight, and continue up to Trow Gill.

Clamber up rocks, and then continue up the steep valley, which
was created by glacial melt-water at the end of an Ice Age, pre-
sumably when Gaping Gill was temporarily blocked. At the top,
cross a ladder stile and take the path which heads towards the
distant summit of Ingleborough.

At a very obvious fork in the path, bear right, which brings

10

you to Gaping Gill. Do take care, especially if you have children or dogs, because this huge swallow-hole can be fatal. There is a direct drop of 104 m.

Now return to the ladder stile, and take the grassy path slightly uphill, to the left of the path by which you arrived.

It starts by heading south, then swings to the east, passing several shake-holes – smaller versions of Gaping Gill, but with no stream to swallow. At a path junction, bear right downhill into a small valley, turn briefly right, then bear left on a path up the other side of the valley.

Take the left hand of two gates at the top, entering Long Lane. After 2.5 km, turn right at a T-junction (CLAPHAM) which will bring you back to the church.

Two ways to shorten the walk

Pay the small toll to walk through the Ingleborough Estate: its old carriage drive is a less demanding ascent, through woods and past an artificial lake.

If the rocky scramble at Trow Gill deters you, return down the path and, just before the toll section, turn left across a footbridge, walking up to Long Lane (see map).

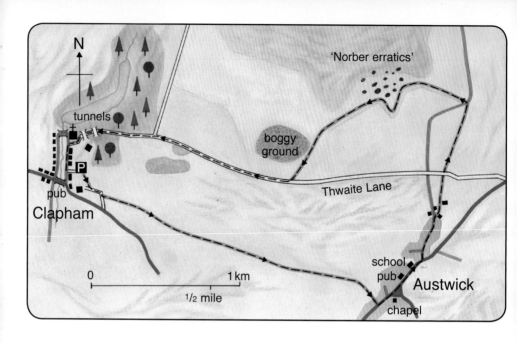

Walk 5   Clapham, Austwick, and the Norber erratics

Distance: 7.3 km (4 1/2 miles)   Time: 2 hours
Character: There are two versions to this walk. If you cut out
the Norber erratics, it is a relatively easy walk of around 6.3 km,
with one short ascent and a few stiles. The full walk adds a fairly
steep ascent, some uneven walking, and a section which might
bother vertigo sufferers – but it takes you into a fascinating
landscape! Could be combined with Walk 6 or Walk 7.

I started from Clapham, but you could equally well start from
Austwick. From the back of the Clapham car park, take PUBLIC
FOOTPATH AUSTWICK. Turn left through a gate, cross the farmyard, and walk along the concrete track. When the track turns
right, continue ahead on the footpath.

   This almost straight, almost flat and (in Summer) well walked
path leads to Austwick. Turn left along the road to the village
centre, and bear left (HORTON) by the church. Pass the Game
Cock Inn and the school, then turn left into TOWNHEAD LANE.

   Walk up the lane, passing Austwick Hall, and then turn right
(by an old milk-churn stand) into a slightly concealed footpath

12

between houses. Continue ahead across a driveway and cross the stile into a field.

Ascend the field and cross a track by two stiles (or turn left along the track for the easy route along Thwaite Lane). Descend the field ahead and then ascend again. Cross directly over the lane onto a footpath (NORBER).

Keep the wall on your right, and watch your step! Cross two stiles and you will enter a field of 'Norber erratics' (see page 15). You may want to explore this area. Otherwise, turn left at the stile and keep the wall on your left, downhill. When you meet a wall ahead of you, turn right, and keep this wall on your left, skirting round the top of the enclosures.

Cross a ladder stile. When the wall ends, continue ahead but slightly to the left, to skirt a boggy area. This should bring you to a ladder stile, which leads into Thwaite Lane. Turn right.

Continue ahead at a junction, and descend through short tunnels into Clapham. At the lane, by the church, turn left. You will find the car park on your left, with a café and a pub a little further along.

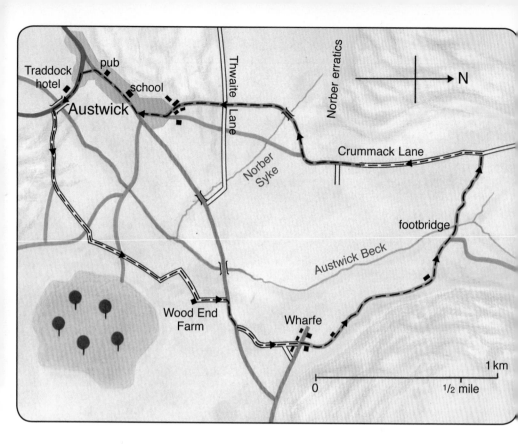

Walk 6 Austwick, Wharfe and Crummackdale

Distance: 6.8km (4¹/4 miles)
Time: 1³/4 hours
Character: A fairly easy walk, mainly using old cart tracks.

Start outside the Game Cock Inn at Austwick and walk downhill to the road junction. Turn left (SETTLE), passing the Traddock hotel. Cross the river bridge and turn left into a metalled track. Follow the enclosed track, cross the PENNINE BRIDLEWAY and continue ahead at the next junction. After a dog-leg, bear left at Wood End Farm, out to a lane.

Turn right, then after 130m bear left on a bridleway. When you reach Wharfe, a pretty hamlet, continue ahead between houses, then bear left and almost immediately turn right on a track past Garth Cottage.

14

The enclosed stony track climbs gently for about 1 km. At a fork, bear left and cross the beck by a narrow stone footbridge. Continue along the enclosed track to a T-junction.

Turn left and follow Crummack Lane back down the valley. When the lane swings right, you could take the footpath across a ladder stile on the left, which is more direct, but if you stay on the quiet lane you will get a closer view of the famous 'Norber erratics' on the skyline. (See Walk 5.)

Descend the lane into the village, passing Austwick Hall, then turn right at the T-junction past the school and back to the Game Cock.

The Norber erratics
These are thousands of large rocks which were carried here from Crummackdale by an Ice Age glacier. When it melted it deposited them a few hundred metres from where they started.

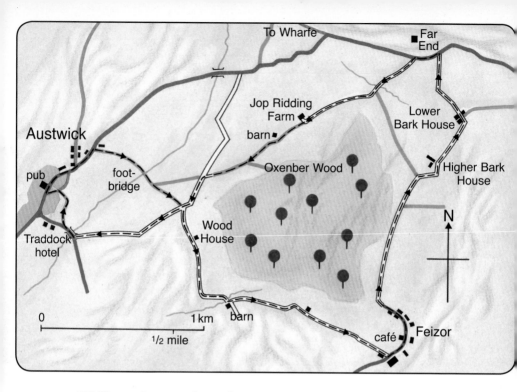

Walk 7 Austwick and Feizor

Distance: 8km (5 miles)   Time: 2 hours
Character: A fairly easy walk, with just one steady climb, using a network of old tracks and droveways.

With your back to Austwick's Game Cock Inn, turn left, passing the school and the foot of TOWNHEAD LANE. After another 150m, turn right beside a barn (PENNINE BRIDLEWAY). Cross a footbridge.

At a track junction, take the middle option (PBW) and continue past a house on your left. After crossing a stream, keep left at the fork, which will bring you to a farmyard at Feizor. Turn left along the lane into the hamlet, past a café.

Keep left at the old pump. The narrow lane begins a long climb up into the limestone, and becomes a track. Once over the top of the ridge, a magnificent view opens up.

Pass Higher Bark House farm (the original barkhouse was probably a medieval tannery belonging to Furness Abbey), then

16

at Lower Bark House turn left (unsigned) through the farmyard and down the access track to a lane. Turn left.

After 150 m turn left on a farm track (FP WOOD LANE) which soon leads gently uphill. At the entrance of Jop Ridding Farm, where the track stops, continue ahead across the field, through a gate and then keep the wall on your right, to cross a ladder stile by a ruined barn.

Again, keep the wall on your right. Cross a stile. (Oxenber Wood on your left is access land as explained on a sign, and well worth exploring, especially for its wild flowers in Spring.) At the foot of a slope, enter an enclosed track, then turn left at the track junction.

You will soon find yourself at a junction you passed earlier: this time cross the PENNINE BRIDLEWAY and continue ahead down the metalled track, which leads to a road. Turn right across the bridge and after 50 m turn right across a stile, onto a footpath which leads between houses. At a lane turn left, which will bring you back to the Game Cock Inn.

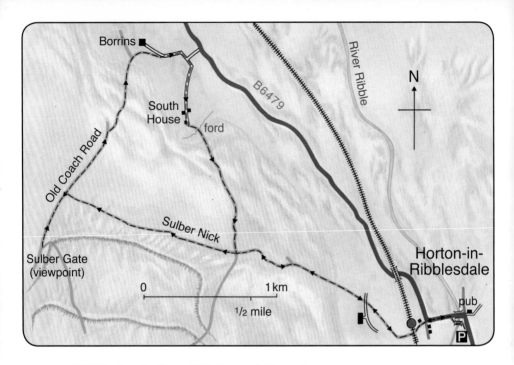

Walk 8   Sulber Nick and Borrins

Distance: 9.7 km (6 miles)   Time: 3 hours
*Character: A gentle steady climb up to a plateau, then an easy
stroll around high pasture – with a short diversion to Sulber
Gate, to view an extraordinary landscape. Compass and map
needed for safety. You could make a good day out by taking a
train to Horton-in-Ribblesdale, but check the timetable first.*

If starting from the car park at Horton, take the footpath in
front of the public conveniences to cross the Ribble by a footbridge, then turn left beside the main road.

Continue ahead to the station, cross the tracks and take the
footpath – it is one of the routes up Ingleborough, so it's well
used. At a path junction with a mini-cairn, turn left as marked.

At the next path junction, continue ahead, INGLEBOROUGH.

Go through a gate into Sulber Nick, a long thin geological
fault line like a shallow valley, where you may be sheltered from
the wind. You will reach a crossroads with a fingerpost: turn left
(PENNINE BRIDLEWAY CLAPHAM) as far as a field gate, from which

18

there is a view over an amazing limestone landscape – and a path down to an the area of limestone pavements (see photo above). It is very easy to lose the path down there, and/or break your ankle, so if you do go down, please take care!

Now retrace your steps to the crossroads and continue ahead on the PENNINE BRIDLEWAY, which in the eighteenth century was actually the main coach road from Lancaster to Newcastle-upon-Tyne. Follow the waymarks to a farm, and go through two gates (SULBER NICK WALK), heading east towards Pen-y-Ghent. Join the farm track.

The waymarks may now cease for a time. At the next track junction, bear right uphill. Follow the track through the farm-yard at South House. Beyond the last barn, bear left through a field gate, and cross a stream. Cross one waymarked stile, but do not head for the next stile! Instead head straight up the slope, where there are waymark posts.

Once at the top, the path becomes clearer, heading roughly south. When you reach a path junction, turn left and retrace your steps down to Horton.

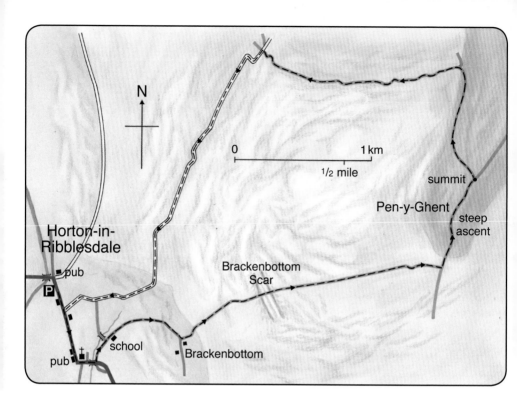

Walk 9 Pen-y-Ghent

Distance: 9.7 km (6 miles) Time: 3 hours
Character: 'Shortish' does not necessarily mean easy, and this one is really strenuous. It involves a climb of 460m (1500ft) and a steep scramble to the summit. Vertigo sufferers may have problems, and the scramble can be slippery in wet or wintery conditions. Compass and map sensible for safety. Pick your day according to the weather.

Alternative version: Most people 'do' Pen-y-Ghent by an easier but longer way – as a there-and-back walk of just under 11 km. Simply reverse the route by which I descended. (But unless you're very sure-footed, don't be tempted to try descending by the steep route!)

Starting from the car park in Horton-in-Ribblesdale (SD 808725), turn right and walk beside the main road to the church. Turn

left (B6479 SETTLE) then take the second turning on the left. Pass the school, then follow this quiet lane to Brackenbottom farm.

Just before a barn, turn left (PEN-Y-GHENT SUMMIT). Go through a pedestrian gate and turn left again. Walk steadily uphill, with a minor scramble at Brackenbottom Scar. When you reach the PENNINE WAY, turn left.

The real ascent starts here, initially steps, then clambering up rocks. It is really steep, exposed to the wind, and vertiginous.

At the summit, turn left over a stile (PENNINE WAY, HORTON-IN-RIBBLESDALE). Before long the path bears right along the top of a scar. At a small cairn, turn left onto a very obvious and well-maintained path and follow it for 1.5km.

At a path junction, turn left (PENNINE WAY, HORTON-IN-RIBBLES-DALE) and follow the enclosed track for 2.5km. At a fork just above the village, bear right downhill to the road. The car park is to your right.

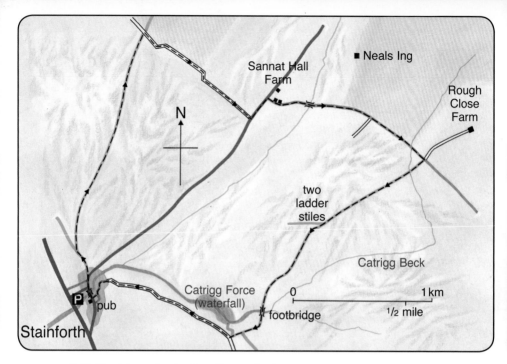

Walk 10   Stainforth and Catrigg Force

Distance: 8.5 km (5¼ miles)   Time: 2¼ hours
Character: A quiet walk in upland pastures, with extensive views,
but also visiting one of the area's more dramatic waterfalls. Two
steep ascents. Compass and map desirable – and you may
actually find the compass useful even in fine weather!

Turn right out of the Stainforth car park, into the village. Turn
left (HALTON GILL) and after 30 m continue ahead up a track
(MOOR HEAD LANE), then ahead again (to the left of Stockhill
House) and then across a stile into fields.

At the first gateway bear right. Climb to a stile at the far right
corner of the field. Now follow a clear path through fields and
a new woodland plantation. At length the path crosses a track.
Turn right along the track and follow it to a lane.

Turn left along the lane. Just before the farm, turn right
(MALHAM) and follow this lane across the beck and steeply up
the other side.

Once over the summit, cross a small stream, then after another

120 m, opposite the entrance to Rough Close, turn right, PUBLIC FOOTPATH STAINFORTH. Cross Catrigg Beck and head west-south-west across rough ground. A row of wooden posts marks the route. There is a slight linear depression, probably a 'holloway' formed by walkers and packhorses over the centuries.

After a stile, head south-west with the wall on your right till you reach two ladder stiles, 25 m apart. Cross the one on the left and, after passing a damp patch, head south-west to a ladder stile. After a further 50 m turn left across another ladder stile, then turn right and keep the wall on your right, crossing the beck by a footbridge. At the far end of the field, turn right across a stone stile and keep the wall on your left to a ladder stile. Cross, and turn right to go through a field gate.

A short diversion signed on the right from this point takes you down to view Catrigg Force waterfall.

Return to the top and turn right along the enclosed track, leading down to Stainforth village. Keep left at the green, then take the first right turn, and right again at the Craven Heifer pub. Turn left at the junction, back to the car park.

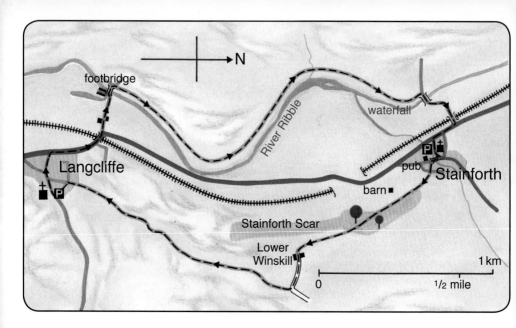

Walk 11   Langcliffe and Stainforth

Distance: 6.6 km (4 miles)   Time: 1 3/4 hours
Character: An easy outward walk along the river valley, then
climbing up to Stainforth, and more steeply up over Stainforth
Scar. There is a pub at the half-way point.

Start from the car park at Langcliffe, opposite the church. Walk
back to the centre of the village and bear right past the war
memorial along NEW STREET, out to the main road. Turn right
along the pavement. Cross the railway and immediately turn
left down a lane.

Just before a terrace of houses, turn right across a footbridge.
On the far side, turn right and right again along the bankside
path. Follow this for 2 km.

At a caravan site, keep right along the bankside path to
Stainforth Force waterfall, then at the bridge turn right and follow the quiet lane up to the main road. Turn right along it.

Take the second road on the left (HALTON GILL), passing a
car park and public toilets. At a T-junction, turn right to cross
Stainforth Beck. Opposite the Craven Heifer turn left (PBW).
Then turn right and immediately left up a track (FP WINSKILL).

24

The River Ribble on the outward route

Looking back to Stainforth Scar as you descend back towards Langcliffe

Go through the upper gate on the far side of the first field. Keep towards the upper side of the next field, with the wood on your left, then go through a gate into the woodland. Climb the steps (which can be slippery after rain) to a ladder stile, emerging on top of the Scar.

The path continues more gently uphill to another ladder stile. Bear left as signed, to a ladder stile at Lower Winskill. Walk through the yard, then ahead up the track for 150 m, and turn right (FP LANGCLIFFE).

Cross a field then after another stile bear right. A clear path now descends, with lovely views in either direction along the valley, ultimately leading to an enclosed track. Follow the track into Langcliffe. At a track junction, bear left, back to the car park.

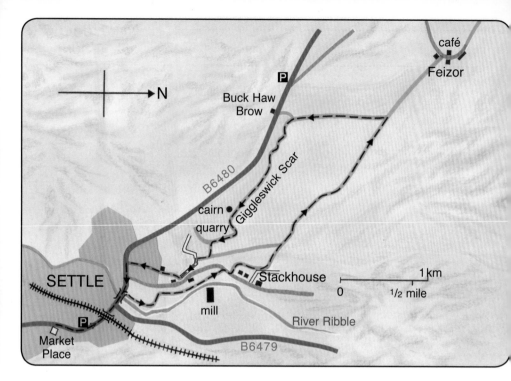

Walk 12   Giggleswick Scar

Distance: 9.7 km (6 miles)   Time: 2¹/₂ hours
Character: Impressive limestone scenery. A moderately easy
walk, though with one steep descent. Can be shortened by
starting from Buck Haw Brow (parking area at SD 792660) and
omitting Settle. Compass and map could be helpful.

From the Market Place at Settle, take the main road north, past
the Royal Oak. Pass the car park, go under the railway viaduct
and cross the river bridge, then immediately turn right on a
footpath (RIBBLE WAY STACKHOUSE).

On reaching a lane turn right along it, and after 200 m bear
left on a footpath (unsigned: go through a pedestrian gate to
access it). Follow the track, with the wall on your right, up to a
track junction. Turn left here at a fingerpost (FEIZOR), away from
the tracks and up a green slope between two mature trees. At the
top of the first slope, bear slightly left which should bring you
to a ladder stile.

26

Go through a gateway on the far side of the next field. Follow a rough track for 200m, then at a horseshoe bend bear right uphill – a short cut, soon rejoining the track. The direct walking route and the meandering track now follow roughly the same north-west direction, which can be a bit confusing.

Follow the track when it turns right through a gate, then immediately left through another gate.

After a long flattish section, you will descend to a path junction. Turn sharp left, BUCK HAW BROW. (Or divert to Feizor, with a café, which is 700m further on.) Walk through fields to a path junction and continue ahead (GIGGLESWICK) and follow the path round to where a dramatic view of the Scar opens up ahead.

Then follow the path as it snakes along with cliffs above and cliffs below. At a cairn, it diverts left to skirt a massive quarry.

At the far side of the quarry, the path begins to swing back to the right. Turn left here, steeply downhill, to join another path and then reach a track. Turn left on the track, through the gate into the wood and then downhill.

At a fork, bear right. This will bring you to a street of bungalows. At its foot, turn left along the main road, back into Settle.

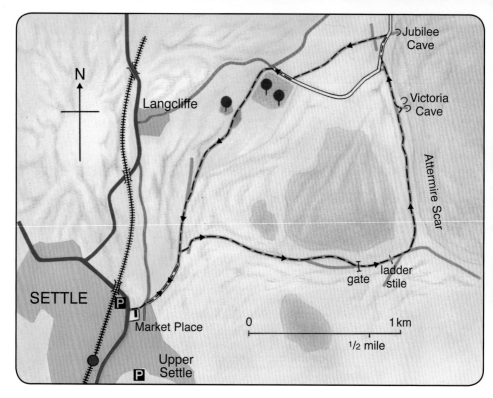

Walk 13   Attermire Scar and Victoria Cave

Distance: 7 km (4¼ miles)   Time: 2 hours
Character: Quite a demanding walk, with two steep ascents,
including one very long ascent at the beginning of the walk. It
passes the entrances to Victoria Cave and Jubilee Cave. Both are
dangerous to enter.

Start from the Market Place at Settle and head uphill from the
north-east corner, signed CASTLEBERG & TOT LORD TRAIL. Keep
left, up CONSTITUTION HILL. After 100 m, bear right up a track
(PENNINE BRIDLEWAY) and climb quite steeply.

   Go through a gate, then after 100 m turn right, PUBLIC FOOT-
PATH MALHAM. Climb very steeply for 50 m, then bear left on a
beaten path, but almost immediately bear right – steeply uphill.
Keep climbing till you reach a wall and continue with the wall
on your left. Follow the broad grassy track to a gate.

   Continue with the wall on your left and keep left when the

28

path forks, though the paths join up again at a gateway. Now head downhill with the wall on your right. Cross a ladder stile.

Continue ahead at a fingerpost. At the end of the cliff swing round to the left. Climb the side valley, then go through a gate in the wall on your right and continue uphill on a stony path. At the top, keep right on a broad grassy track.

You will pass Victoria Cave on your right. There is a helpful information board just outside the cave.

Continue along the main path till you reach a farm track, and continue ahead along it to the mouths of Jubilee Cave, to the right of the track.

After looking at the entrances, retrace your steps for 50 m, cross the track and cross the ladder stile ahead of you. Go straight ahead at a path crossroads. Head initially west then south-west, descending till you rejoin the farm track by a wood. Turn right down to a lane junction. Turn left here through a gate, PENNINE BRIDLEWAY SETTLE.

Follow the beaten path through a series of gates, pastures and a droveway. After a gate, keep the wall on your right, heading almost south. After a while you will find yourself retracing your steps back down to Settle.

The Ingleton Falls walk

Ingleton has a famous waterfall walk, including Thornton Force (photo above). The walk doesn't meet the criteria for this book because there's a significant admission charge (the path and bridges are expensive to maintain) but it can be recommended, especially after rain when the falls are at their best.

The Peaks

'Shortish' walks are supposed to be circular and under 9km in length, and none of the Three Peaks can be climbed under those criteria – though we have included the circular Pen-y-Ghent walk (Walk 9) because it is only slightly too long and a great walk.

For Ingleborough, a circular walk would be far too long, so we are including the there-and-back walk from Ingleton.

The routes from Clapham (an extension of Walk 4) and from Horton (an extension of Walk 8) are slightly longer, but perhaps a little easier.

For Whernside, we recommend a there-and-back walk from the Blea Moor side, starting from Ribblehead.

For all three peaks, choose a clear day, with a light wind, and be sure to take water, refreshments, and several extra layers of clothing: it is amazing how much colder and windier it can be up there. The routes are navigationally easy, but you should still take a map and compass for safety.

Ingleborough from Ingleton

Distance: 11 km (6³/4 miles)   Time: 4 hours
A strenuous walk, ascending and descending 610 m (2000 ft) and quite uneven underfoot for much of the way – but fantastic scenery and a sense of achievement when you reach the summit!

Start from the main (Community Centre) car park. From the end furthest from the village centre, turn left (B6255 HAWES). At the top of the slope, keep right and at the next junction keep left, HAWES. After a further 130 m, bear right up a track (FP INGLEBOROUGH) and follow it out onto the open moor.

Keep right, as signed, at Crina Bottom farm (see photo below). When you think you've arrived at the top, sorry, you haven't! There are several false summits.

Ribblehead viaduct at the start of the walk, with Whernside behind it

Approaching the summit of Whernside, where the ground to either side of the path is peat bog, and this tarn is a distinctive landmark

Whernside from Ribblehead

Distance: 13.7 km (8 1/2 miles)   Time: 4 hours
A long haul, ascending and descending 450 m (1500 ft) and uneven underfoot for much of the way. Although Whernside is less dramatic than the other two peaks, it is still a fine walk.

Start as for Walk 2, but continue ahead on the main path, past Blea Moor signal box. After crossing the railway, keep left, DENT DALE. After a further 850 m, turn left over a stile (WHERNSIDE) and follow the well maintained path over what would otherwise be peat bog to the summit, at 736 m.